What I See, I Can Be
A Guided Yoga Flow for Children

Author

Janet Williams

Illustrations
Korey McCumber (drawings and line work)
Mark Stanleigh (colouring and design)

This book is dedicated to all children.
They have the ability to see magic in the world, with their fresh eyes and open hearts.

Special thanks to my friend Gratia, who inspired me to write this book,
the fantastic and talented artists Korey McCumber and Mark Stanleigh, who made this project so much fun,
my loving spouse Michael, who encouraged me throughout the whole long process,
and to all of my dear family and friends, who believed in me and the benefits of this wonderful book,
thank you from the bottom of my heart.

Light & Love
Janet Williams

Light Connections Press
Committed to Children's Health and Caring for the Environment

Text and Illustrations ©2009 by Author Janet Olwen Williams
Illustrations: Linework and drawings by Korey McCumber. Colour and design by Mark Stanleigh.

For information, please contact Janet Williams at info@ChildrensYogaBooks.com

Published by *Light Connections Press*
Committed to Children's Health and Caring for the Environment.
5082 Parkplace Circle, Mississauga, Ontario, Canada, L5V 2M1
First Edition. Printed in Canada.

See our complete product line at www.ChildrensYogaBooks.com
Light Connections Press offers special discounts for bulk purchases.
For more information, please contact us at: www.ChildrensYogaBooks.com

Disclaimer: You are responsible for your own body and for the choices you make regarding the stretches described in this book. We will not be held responsible for any injuries that may occur.

Library and Archives Canada Cataloguing in Publication

Williams, Janet, 1968-
    What I see, I can be : a guided yoga flow for children / Janet Williams ; [illustrated by Korey McCumber and Mark Stanleigh].

Accompanied by audio CD.
For ages 3-9.
ISBN 978-0-9810902-1-4

    1. Hatha yoga--Juvenile literature. I. McCumber, Korey, 1980- II. Stanleigh, Mark, 1987-
III. Title.

RA781.7.W54 2009   j613.7'046   C2009-902740-2

Production management by TRIMATRIX Management Consulting Inc.
TRIMATRIX assumes no responsibility for damages, direct or indirect, from publication of the included works. Work is included as provided by the author, views expressed are those of the author and any errors, omissions or otherwise are the author's responsibility. (www.trimatrixmanagement.com)

Mixed Sources
Cert no. SW-COC-001271
© 1996 FSC

Teachers, Parents, and Caregivers: How to Use this Book

What I See, I Can Be: A Guided Yoga Flow for Children is a "how to" Yoga Book for children with a storybook twist. As children learn the yoga names and body movements for each of the postures, they are encouraged to engage their imaginations by visualizing the creative scenes the postures are set in. This interactive book allows parents and teachers to guide children through a standard yoga workout. As you read the story, have the children emulate Julie and Andy, the two children in the book who model the yoga postures and stretches. Children should be encouraged to breathe slowly and deeply and to stretch only as far as it feels comfortable for their body.

Yoga awakens the body's flexibility, strength and balance and simultaneously improves the mind's ability to focus. Children experience the benefits of releasing tension, relaxing their bodies and improving their concentration abilities, which are just some of the benefits of practicing yoga. Yoga is good any time of day. At the start of each day, teachers can have children do a yoga workout to help prepare their bodies and minds to focus on the rest of the day's activities. At the end of each day, in preparation for bedtime, parents can have children do a yoga session in order to stretch out any physical tension, to relax the body and to help quiet the mind. Once children become familiar with the book, they can use their imaginations to create their own stretches and postures because What They See, They Can Be.

-Janet Williams

When, Where and Why to Use this Book in the Classroom:
The Versatility of this Resource

Finally, a yoga resource that is effective, easy to follow, and fully inclusive of all physical ability levels!
The book is perfect to use for yoga outdoors. Both the book and CD will rapidly become valuable and essential components of a high quality DPA program. Teachers in open concept classrooms will find that the CD works wonderfully when played at normal teacher volume with the children following along.
Use the CD to do a few poses after periods of high activity to bring the mind and body back to a place of focus and calm – allowing for optimal learning to take place! This is an irreplaceable DPA resource that every Primary/Junior teacher should own.

-Suki McVeety, DPA Coordinator, Grade 4/5 Teacher, Peel School Board and Parent of a 5 and 9 year old

What I See, I Can Be. I see a Mountain. I can be a Mountain, stretching high into the sky.

I plant my feet into the ground and make my shoulders big and broad.
I lift my arms into the sky and feel my fingertips stretching through the clouds.
I relax my body and stand very straight and still.
I breathe very deeply and, as I breathe out, I move the clouds with my breath.
I am a Mountain.

What I See, I Can Be. I see a Tree. I can be a Tree, standing tall and true.

I place one foot on my lower leg to make a sturdy tree trunk.
I grow roots from the bottom of my foot deep into the earth.
My arms come up like branches reaching up into the sunlight.
Sometimes as I breathe, my branches sway in the breeze.
I am a Tree.

What I See, I Can Be. I see a Kite in the shape of a triangle. I can be a Kite, soaring across the sky, first to the right and then to the left.

I place my feet far apart and, stretching my arms out to the sides, I make kite wings. I turn my right foot out and point it in the same direction as my right hand. I feel the wind gently moving my right hand over as far as I can reach.

Then I gracefully swoop my right hand to the ground. I keep my arms nice and straight as I glide close to the earth. The wind slowly raises my right hand up. Then I turn my left foot out and gently stretch my left hand far to the side. The wind brings my hand down to the earth and my arms are straight as I soar. Then, I happily swoop my arm back up again as the wind pushes me up. I am a Kite.

What I See, I Can Be. I see a Dog. I can be a Dog, stretching my body after waking up from a nap.

I place my hands on the ground far away from my feet.
My front paws are flat on the ground, and I allow my heels to lower slowly
to the earth.
I feel my tail reach for the sky and my dog ears reach between my elbows.
I imagine that I can wag my tail to show that I am happy to be awake.
I am a Dog.

What I See, I Can Be. I see a Cat. I can be a Cat, arching its furry back.

I put my hands and knees on the ground.
My hands are under my shoulders and my knees are under my hips.
My back is very straight and so are the whiskers on my face.

As I breathe in, my furry belly fills with air and my whiskers face up.
As I breathe out, I arch my cat back to the sky and my whiskers are face down.
I breathe nice and slowly and move my back up and down.
I am a Cat.

What I See, I Can Be. I see a Mouse. I can be a Mouse, quiet and small.

I kneel on the earth and I cover my knees with my chest.
My forehead touches the ground and my hands stretch out in front of me.
I feel my thin, long tail resting on my feet, and I breathe very slowly and softly.
As quiet as a mouse, I move my hands behind me.
I curl myself up, and I feel my back rising and falling as I breathe.
I am a Mouse.

What I See, I Can Be. I see a Cobra. I can be a Cobra, majestic and strong.

I lie on my stomach and make myself long by bringing my feet and knees close together. I place my hands on the earth under my shoulders.
I touch the ground very gently with my forehead, and then my nose, and then my chin.

I come up slowly like a majestic cobra.
When my head is all the way up, I flicker my snake tongue very quickly.
I am a Cobra.
Then, I slowly lower my head and gently touch my chin to the earth, and then my nose, and then my forehead.
I make a pillow with my hands and rest my head and I breathe.

What I See, I Can Be. I see a Boat. I can be a Boat, sailing through the water on a sunny day.

Lying on my stomach, I stretch my arms straight out in front of me.
I take a deep breath in, and I lift my arms into the air to make the bow of the boat.

I lift my legs into the air to make the stern of the boat.
My belly is floating on the water and my arms and legs stay high and dry.
I wiggle my fingers and toes in the air and I move my sails into the wind.
I smile as I sail through the clear, blue water.
I am a Boat.

What I See, I Can Be. I see a Bridge. I can be a Drawbridge, lifting up to let ships go by.

I lie on my back and I place my feet on the ground.
I bring my feet close to my bottom and my knees point to the sky.
A ship is ready to leave the harbour and head out to sea.

I put my hands on my back and lift my tummy high into the air.
I breathe as the ship slowly sails under the bridge.
I am a Bridge.
When the ship is through, I slowly lower the Drawbridge by bringing my back flat onto the ground.

What I See, I Can Be. I see a Bow and Arrow. I can be a mighty Bow, flexible and strong.

Lying on my stomach, I bend my knees.
My hands reach behind to hold on to my feet or pants.
I hold on tightly and lift my hands and feet higher into the air, which makes my bow very strong and steady.
Sometimes I rock back and forth as I breathe.
I am a Bow.

What I See, I Can Be. I see a Tortoise. I can be a Tortoise inside my sturdy, grey shell.

I put my legs out in front of me and I lift my knees.
I push my hands under my knees. I curl my back and extend my
head out of my shell by bringing my chest close to the earth.
I relax in the bright sun and I feel the sunshine warming my back.
I am a Tortoise.

What I See, I Can Be. I see an Oyster. I can be an Oyster, making a pearl when I close.

I bring my legs together and place one tiny grain of sand on my soft belly.

I raise my arms above my head, which makes the top half of my shell.

I slowly begin to close by stretching my hands close to my ankles or toes.

I breathe deeply into my soft belly, and I begin to wrap the grain of sand with my special stomach juices. As I breathe, the pearl becomes bigger, and I wrap more and more of my special coating around it. When I am ready, I slowly lift my arms to open my shell. My beautiful pearl shines brightly in the sun. I am an Oyster with a radiant pearl. I leave my precious pearl on my stomach, and I lie on my back, opening up fully to the sun.

What I See, I Can Be. I see a Meadow. I can be a Meadow by lying down and closing my eyes.
I squeeze the muscles in my feet and legs. Then I relax by letting my toes hang out to the sides. I squeeze the muscles in my arms and lift them slightly off the ground, and I make my fists into two tight balls.
Then I relax my arms and let them rest away from my body.

I open my hands so that my palms are facing the sky. I squeeze, squeeze,
squeeze my shoulders up to my ears, and then I relax my shoulders.
I squeeze my face into a tight little ball, as if I have just eaten a lemon.
Then I relax my face and keep my eyes closed.
My tummy goes up and down as I breathe, which moves the meadow grass
in the breeze. I listen to the meadow sounds.

I hear the chirping of birds in the air and the swimming of fish
in the stream. I watch a white cloud float by.
A colourful butterfly flutters around me.

I imagine I can see fairies playing in the meadow.
I continue to breathe until my body and mind are calm and relaxed.
I am a Meadow.

About the Author

Janet Williams is a Yoga Instructor and a certified Primary-Junior School Teacher. She has studied Hatha Yoga in Canada, Australia, England and Spain. Janet has studied and learned different yoga disciplines including Kripalu, Iyengar, Sivananda and Kundalini. She has been practicing yoga since 1988 and has been teaching yoga since 1996. Janet is the owner of Body Light™, which focuses on Yoga, Goal Setting, Healing and Self Discovery, by utilizing the unique Body Light™ Wellness System.

For more information, visit us at *www.ChildrensYogaBooks.com*